The Human Character

Tell Your Story Using Amazon.com

Graeme Smith

PUBLISHED ON AMAZON.COM
BY
LABYRINTH BOOKS

DEDICATION:

This book is dedicated to my family.
    Hele-ly (Ly).
        my wife:

    Ingrid.
        our daughter:

    Marie.
        my former wife:

    Fiona, Natalie and Michael
        our children:

    Georgie
        Michael's wife:

    Pearl, Kiki and Martha.
        their children:

They have put up with me for many years and I thank them for that.
I hope this book gives an insight into what occupied me much of the time.
All have done worthwhile and interesting things in the absence of my help.
I congratulate them for their achievements.

HOW TO USE Tell Your Story.

Usually people don't think through things to the level they need to.
Because of that, they have projects instead of tasks on their "to do" list.
That leads to procrastination for it hasn't been broken down to a task level.

START at the PART of the book that interests you MOST.
Make notes of the steps you will need to take and resources required.
Use notes to create a step by step system for implementing ideas.
Often you won't refer back to an original if you've created **YOUR** system.

The first question to ask and answer is "Why is this being done?"
Define it - what is success for this project and how will you know?

Brainstorm all the tasks are involved in your project.
It's important not to go linear too fast with this.
By linear, I mean step one, step two, step three, and step four.
As you plan step one, two, three, there is a specific step that might be four.
Start steps too quickly, other ways for one, two and three may not appear.

The first third of a brainstorming session is easy - find lots of ideas.
The second third is challenging – look at the ideas to see where they go.
Push to think outside the box for that's often where the big idea is!
That's where the most powerful way of getting a project done the fastest is.

Once you've brainstormed a project put options in a linear sequence.
Then figure out what you've overlooked and all becomes obvious.
Get tasks in order, add missing steps, and lay out your list for the project.

When you've organized the tasks into a linear process decide:
What can you start immediately?

What can start that is not dependent on things that must occur beforehand?

Get started on them right away!

Write things you think of and cross off things as you do them.

TELL YOUR STORY.

INDEX:

A: AMAZON.COM:

Build your book.

Have TWO files for your book.

Initially use a MS Word file.
This is where you do **ALL** your writing **AND** editing.
BUT you do not have any formatting problems.

Before entering anything at all:
Decide what font you want to use (mine is Arial).
Decide what size print you want as well.
I use 10 point with 12 for headings.
Adjust these to get what you are happy with.

Download Kindle.Create.
Build a template of paragraph headings in your Kindle Create file.

The first page to complete is the DETAILS page.
Here you provide your language.

ALSO:
Enter **EXACTLY** your book title.
Enter **EXACTLY** your book sub-title.
Enter **EXACTLY** your name.

These details ALWAYS MUST be entered EXACTLY the same way.
Otherwise you will **NOT** be able to access your book.
They allow you to check what you have entered whenever required.

So write down what you entered - exactly.

You can complete other book details later, many of which can be changed.

The rest of that first page is for use by Amazon.com too.
It's how Amazon.com keeps track of your book.
Most (but not all) of this information can be changed later (any time).

Spend time getting the Amazon details page right.
Amazon will provide comments about things that need fixing.
You then fix the problem(s).
Eventually the Amazon details page is correct.

NOW enter your main thoughts.
They might become headings for the chapters of your book.
Then they automatically become paragraphs in your book.
Page numbering is automatic too.
They also become your Table of Contents.

Actual chapters still need to be written.
Write in your MS Word file and later they can be copied into Kindle.Create.

Naturally I do not know your story.
So I have used one of my books to illustrate what you might do.

This is the title of one of my books.
MY MEMORIES

The subheading is:
Some thoughts.

A Table of Contents is automatically created.
So you do not need to compile that.
BUT you **DO** need to decide where you want it.

You can also decide what you want to call it.
Possibly INDEX or just CONTENTS.
Otherwise it will be TABLE OF CONTENTS.

The description is a VERY important piece of information.
You are allowed 4000 words **AND** this includes spaces.

Exactly what you write is available for anyone to read.
You are **NOT** told this.

Amazon.com uses this information to SELL your book.
That means what you put there **MUST** be a sales message.
NOT just something about the book.

Potential buyers read this when they decide whether to buy or not.
BUT this message now only has a space between each line.

So write your message that way too.
Then readers will read what you want them to.
The way you want them to.

This sales message can be changed at any time.
You might need a different message if you have sold many books.
Or perhaps if you have a discount promotion.
Or you just think of a better way to do it!

You can put the sales message on the back cover of your book too.
Do that when you are creating your cover.
But this time write it as a normal text message.
Then anyone picking up a printed book is exposed to your sales message.

Getting your manuscript right can be done over time.
So update the manuscript as many times as necessary.
An updated book usually takes about 2 days to re-appear.

If it is just to your text it is quicker.

B: TELL YOUR STORY.

Maybe writing is NOT what you do much.

Just some words on a mobile phone.
Or a text message.
Probably you've never previously thought about writing a book either.

Writing is about communication.
So what is communication?
It's not just sending messages.
It's **NOT** what Alexander Graham Bell would have thought either.

Communication is about sending AND receiving messages.
The message sent and received should be the same.
Or at least very similar.
The smaller the difference the better the communication.

There are many ways to communicate.
How I have done it has changed over the years too.
Books are my latest and probably last version.

It's not just a matter of writing or saying stuff either.
It has to be in a way that the target for the communication understands.
There are jokes about poor communication between males and females.

We all start quite naturally and then get educated!
Eventually some people go to university and such places.
There they learn academic forms of communication.

I've even used academic communication.
It's more formal and intended for people who are used to its conventions.
With references, quotes and various words with specific meanings.

The last time I did this in the mid 1970's when I wrote a philosophical essay.

BUT I've written a great deal that was not for academics.
My audience has been teachers, artists, art buyers and business people.

Recently I've been discussing topics on LinkedIn.
Some of the people with whom I discuss questions are academics.
You can tell by the letters after their name or Dr in front of it.
But even without that their language is a give-away.

In quite a few cases I find I can't understand what they write.
I have to ask them to write more simply.

In turn they sometimes dismiss what I write.
Because I haven't used their language conventions.
But I learned academic writing too, when I attended university.

Start your book by recording some thoughts.
Get them down before they disappear.
Do **NOT** worry about how they are written.

If necessary get someone to translate this into a written format.
Then add more thoughts.

Keep going like this and eventually you'll have a book.
It will sound like you too.
Because it is the same words you use.
In the same way.

The main thing is for your style to be consistent.
BUT if it's always you talking then your style **IS** consistent.

So writing a book is actually the easy part.
Just do it in a series of small steps.
YOU are responsible for what is written **NOT** Amazon.com.

Publishing your story is different.
But this book helps you with that.

Promoting your book is actually the most difficult aspect of all.
TELL YOUR STORY helps you there too (a later chapter).

Amazon.com offers some error correcting.
But it accepts the style you use.

Amazon.com accepts whatever you actually write too.
This is a major difference from book publishers.
There your book **MUST** be right **BEFORE** it is published!

The start stops most people.

Back in my art student days I learnt how to deal with this problem.
I was in the third year of a four-year art course.
One evening I arrived for his class to find I was the only person there!

I wasn't happy but decided not to waste my time.
I also found the solution to that particular problem.
Just start!

You can learn from my experience.
It doesn't matter what you do at the start, as long as you do something.
It can be random.'
But that doesn't necessarily have to be the case.

TELL YOUR STORY is so you do something similar.
BUT it will not be the same.
For I had **NO** instructions!

Also I made LOTS of mistakes.
I tried many solutions to the problems I faced.

Learn what I learned!
Do **NOT** do what I did to learn it though!
For then you will make the same mistakes I did!

So don't wait, get on with it - just get started!
Then your imagination can work for you!

Some of my story.

I live in Wagga Wagga in Australia.
I've lived here since 1977.
So I'm comfortable with this city of around 65,000 people.
It's an environment with both strengths and weaknesses.

I'm not located in the major art centres of my country.
So I'm out of touch with the current art scene there.
But the conventional wisdoms don't seem to work for many artists.
I'm independent and provide an alternative for those who need it.

In recent years, e-mail eliminates distance dramatically.
So I am in touch with artists all over the world.
This refreshes and renews my thinking.
I've also found that the art culture is much the same everywhere.
I find there is interest in my views as a result.

Tell Your Story is so your experience is similar.
BUT it will not be the same.
For I had **NO** instructions!

Also I made LOTS of mistakes.
I tried many solutions to the problems I faced.
But often the solution came years after it was needed.

Practice and theory go hand in hand.
There are things for you to do as well as explanations.

Doing something Is a better way to understand art than reading.
You meet the essence of Tell Your Story at the start.

Remember learn what I learned!
NOT what I did to learn it though!
Then you'd make the same mistakes as me.

C: PUBLISH:

KINDLE CREATE.

Kindle Create is a tool from Amazon.com.
It helps you format your finished manuscript.
Then turn it into an attractive eBook.

Import to Amazon a manuscript in the .doc/.docx format.
Kindle Create automatically detects chapter titles.
It adds styling to them, and create a table of contents.
In addition, you can format individual paragraphs.
Using styles like first paragraph with drop caps or block quotes.

There are a variety of visual book layout themes.
Select one to match the tone of your story.
You can also preview how your book will look on devices and apps.

Kindle Create currently supports books in these languages.
English, French, Italian, German, Spanish, Portuguese and Dutch.
To change the language setting, click Help.
Then "Set Up Language" to choose your preferred language.

To learn more about Kindle Create.
Go to Help at:
https://kdp.Amazon.com/help/topic/GHU4YEWXQGNLU94T

If you approach it as you might for any other publisher.
Publishing with Amazon.com can seem hard.

You can see all the publishing tools Amazon.com offers.
Compare them at this link:
https://kdp.Amazon.com/en_US/help/topic/A3IWA2TQYMZ5J6

Here's how to start a book with Amazon:

Install and open an Amazon.com account.
Go to Amazon Kindle Direct Publishing.
Follow the prompts to register.

Once you are registered select "Choose File".
This opens your book file.

Now open your bookshelf.
Click on Create a New Title (upper left)

Commence with a paperback book.
After that you can download to a Kindle ebook easily.

Spend time getting the Amazon details page right.
Eventually the Amazon details page is correct.
Then go to the next page.

Scroll down and then click:
"Upload paperback manuscript" to upload your content.
Browse to the revised file of your book content and click to upload.
When you've uploaded a paperback update, click "Approve."

Go to "Cover Creator" to create or change the cover.
Click "Save and Continue" to go to the "Paperback Rights & Pricing" page.
If you've uploaded a paperback update click "Approve."
Click "Publish" at the bottom of the page.

Interior: Book details:
Make sure the information in your interior and cover files exactly match.
The book details (e.g., title, author name, ISBN, language)

Compare the book details you entered **during title setup.**

With the information in your manuscript and on your cover.

Be sure to check all locations where book details appear.
For example copyright page, headers, etc.
The information in your interior and cover files **MUST** <u>exactly</u> match.

If the details in your manuscript file don't match.
Correct any differences, including minor ones.
Like author name John T. Smith in book details and J.T. Smith on title page.
Check all locations where book details appear (copyright page, headers).
Update your book details or upload your revised file to KDP.

To edit a previously published book.
Click the ellipsis button ("…") next to the book you want to edit.
Select "Edit Paperback Content."

Amazon.com is NOT the same as other publishers.

Initially Amazon only published ebooks.
They are electronic books.
There is **NO** actual printed material.

The Amzon.com eBook system was later adapted for printed books.
A later innovation is different paths for novels and text/reference books.
My books were published before that.

A publisher publishes AND sells books.
Publishers earn money by selling books.

When printed a book can't be changed.
Editing is done **BEFORE** publication.

Amazon.com also publishes physical books.
BUT they are printed versions of eBooks.

So Amazon.com book publishing is different.
It's based on the eBook system Amazon.com uses.
Thus Amazon.com sells titles **NOT** books.

Which means EVERYTHING is ELECTRONIC.
Amazon.com has a huge store of electronic books.

There are advantages for authors as a result.
That's if you know of and use the opportunities provided.
Tell Your Story helps you do this.

Rights.
You keep control of your rights and set your own list prices.
You can make changes to your books at any time.

Earn up to 70% royalty on sales to:

US, Canada, UK, Germany, India, France, Italy, Spain, Japan, Brazil, Mexico, Australia and more.

You might enroll in KDP Select.

Earn money in Kindle Unlimited and the Kindle Owners' Lending Library.

OWN COVER:

You can design a new cover using the Cover Creator tool:
These covers includes the spine and back page.
ALL my covers used Amazon.com's cover creator tool.

Sign in to kdp.Amazon.com and go to your Bookshelf
Click on an existing book title or create a new title

In the eBook Content or Paperback Content tab.
Scroll down to the Cover section and click "Launch Cover Creator".
The tool will open and instruct you how to proceed.

When uploading your own cover file.
Be sure to upload it as one continuous image in a PDF file.
Also include the front cover, back cover, and spine.

Edit the details of any previously published cover image.
Then submit the revised cover image in PDF for your book.

Use blank template or template with sample content for your trim size.
Templates with sample content include:
Front matter, chapters, headers, and page numbers.

If you're copying and pasting from an existing document.
All templates are adjustable to your preferences or book specifications.

Cover formatting guide with tips for avoiding common file rejections:
https://kdp.Amazon.com/help/topic/G201953020

To learn more, check Help and watch a short video:
https://kdp.Amazon.com/help/topic/A1DO53V18UNF0M

It is NOT possible to edit the details of the cover image.
Of a previously published book for your new book.
Using Amazon.com's publishing tools.

If it's NOT possible to edit the cover image.
Amazon.com can help.

Make sure you hold all appropriate rights to use any image.
It must meet one of the following requirements:
TIFF (.tif/.tiff) or JPEG (.jpeg/.jpg) format.

Size your cover so it includes your book's trim size, spine width.
AND at least 0.125" (3 mm) of bleed, centered horizontally and vertically.

Ideal dimensions for cover files:
2,560 pixels in height x 1,600 pixels in width.
Minimum dimensions of 1000 pixels in height and 625 pixels in width.
Minimum 72 dpi (dots per inch), with 300 dpi being ideal.

RGB color profile.
For best quality, particularly on high definition devices.
Your image should be: 2500 pixels in height

Amazon.com can't accept images larger than 10,000 pixels in height.
After you upload your image and click "Save and Publish,"
The changes will show up on the website within 72 hours.

SAVING IMAGE:

To design a new cover using Cover Creator:
Sign in to kdp.Amazon.com and go to your Bookshelf.
Click on an existing title or create a new title.
In the eBook Content or Paperback Content tab.
Scroll down to the Cover section and click "Launch Cover Creator".
The tool will open and instruct you how to proceed.

To learn more, check Help and watch a short video:
https://kdp.Amazon.com/help/topic/A1DO53V18UNF0M

You can also check out KDP University, for more resources:
https://kdp.Amazon.com/en_US/help/topic/G200783400

Make sure you hold all appropriate rights to use images.
Also, check your cover meets the following requirements:
Size all images at 100% and flatten to one layer

Minimum image resolution must be 300 DPI (dots per inch).
Cover text is 7-point font, isn't cut off, or overlapped by other elements.
And doesn't blend into the background.

How to save an image as JPEG/TIF.
Open Paint.
Paint comes pre-installed on your PC.
Open your image in Paint.
Make sure the image is on your computer.

Click "File," then click the arrow next to "Save As."
A list of image types, including JPEG, will appear.
Click "JPEG."
Rename the file if you wish, then click "Save."

For paperback book Covers JPEG or TIF is not a supported format.
You need to create the paperback cover in PDF.

For best results when creating your paperback cover.
Format using an Amazon.com template:
https://kdp.Amazon.com/cover-templates

To calculate a cover size, downloading File Setup Calculator.
On https://kdp.Amazon.com/help/topic/A1L46HVPPIYTE
Under the "Cover size" section.

Or follow these guidelines:
Minimum cover width = bleed + back cover width trim size + spine width.
+ front cover width trim size + bleed.
Minimum cover height = bleed + book height trim size + bleed.

To calculate spine width for black ink books:
White paper: multiply page count by 0.002252" (0.0572 mm).
Cream paper: multiply page count by 0.0025" (0.0635 mm).

To calculate spine width for color ink books:
Multiply page count by 0.002347" (0.0596 mm).

Expected size of the cover is 12.892x 9.250.
But uploaded cover is 6.000x9.000.
The easiest solution is to use the cover templates:
Templates help create print-ready covers for your book.

To get started using Amazon.com templates:
Sign in to http://kdp.Amazon.com
Go to https://kdp.Amazon.com/cover-templates

Configure your template.
Select the trim size, number of pages, and paper color for your book

Click "Download Cover Template"
Follow the instructions on the Help page for how to use your template.

Open the zip file for the book cover template there are two files.
Both contain the same content, but are opened with different programs.
These files can be used with a variety of image editing software.
Such as, Adobe Photoshop and Adobe InDesign, among others.

You only need to use the file type (.png or PDF).
Whichever corresponds with the appropriate editing software.

To accurately calculate the size of the cover.
Before creating the cover use Amazon.com's file calculator.

To calculate your cover size, download File Setup Calculator
https://images-na.ssl-images-
Amazon.com/images/G/01/00/00/99/81/32/06/9981320610.xlsm
Open the calculator (all of the above).

MORE INFORMATION:

For more information on designing your cover, visit the help page:
https://kdp.Amazon.com/help?topicId=A1L46HVPPIYTE

Check out KDP University, for more resources:
https://kdp.Amazon.com/en_US/help/topic/G200783400

To update your cover:
Follow the instructions below.
Title, subtitle, author name, and series information on your cover.
Match the book details you entered.

Go to your Bookshelf
Click the ellipsis button ("…") under KINDLE EBOOK ACTIONS.
OR
PAPERBACK ACTIONS next to the book you want to update.

Choose Edit eBook content or Edit paperback content.
This takes you to the Content page.
Scroll down to the "Cover" section.

Choose Launch Cover Creator.
OR
Upload your cover file to update your cover
OR
Upload a cover you already have.

Once the content completes the upload process.
The message "Cover uploaded successfully" will appear.
The conversion process will start.
This can take several minutes depending on the complexity of the file).

Go to the "Kindle eBook Preview" or "Book Preview" section.
Click Launch Previewer.

Make sure your updated cover looks as expected
Before saving in pdf is the Book and cover set out correctly?
Each page must be correct.
You need to do this.

Click Save and continue.
This takes you to the Pricing page

Click the publish button at the bottom of this page
Update book details.
title, description, categories, manuscript, cover, publishing territory rights.
Amazon.com reviews to meet guidelines for details, content, and quality.

Learn more about timelines for updates to published books.

D: PROMOTE:

MARKETING:

Start publishing your book by considering the marketing first.
That's because marketing is the most difficult aspect to do properly.

By planning your promotion early.
Your book can be written to take advantage of opportunities offered.

One opportunity is how Amazon keeps track of your book?
Amazon.com has a huge store of electronic books.

When first published they allocate ASIN numbers to your book.
Every book published by Amazon.com has a unique ASIN number.
Each ASIN number has TEN digits.

Most have TWO ASIN numbers.
One if for ebooks.
The other is for Paperback books.

ASIN numbers link to the details you entered but now can't change.
Your book title.
Your book sub-title.
Your name.

That's why they ALWAYS MUST be entered EXACTLY the same way.
Otherwise you will **NOT** be able to access your book.

So make sure you write down what you entered.
You can complete other book details later as many can be changed.

ASIN numbers also link to other details you entered.
The book description or sales message is one of them.

This sales message can be changed at any time.
You might need a different message if you have sold many books.
Or perhaps if you have a discount promotion.

If people click on an ASIN number they go to Amazon.com sales page.
This is when they decide whether to buy or not.
Potential buyers can read the sales message.
They also find out the book price.

So a link to an ASIN number is the BEST way to market a book.
Then anyone who receives that can actually **BUY** your book.

So how do you know what the ASIN numbers are?
They are on your bookshelf.
There you will see TWO ASIN numbers.
One if for Kindle books and the other for Paperback books.

Copy the ASIN numbers to send to prospective buyers.
BUT you can't do that until your book is published?
So what do you do?

What if you haven't published your book yet?
Then you do not have any ASIN numbers.
In fact you do not yet have a book.

Use a temporary reminder.
When writing your book enter a dummy link where you want it to be.

So publish your book as soon as you can.
Then you have ASIN numbers to insert in your book.
You can also use them elsewhere too.

Once you have your FINAL manuscript.
THEN publish your book.

AS SOON AS it is published.
Go to your bookshelf and copy the correct ASIN Numbers.
Enter these instead of your temporary/false numbers.

Then republish your book.
It is **NOW** a correct version.

Do this as soon as possible.
Before anyone buys a book with the wrong numbers.

No-one is going to buy your book if they don't know about it.
So **AVOID** actually promoting your book.
Do this when everything else has been done.

Later you can even use Facebook to promote your book.
Just copy the book link into Facebook.
Anyone clicking the link is taken to the sales page.
Then they can decide for themselves whether to buy or not.

SELL MORE BOOKS:

People who buy your book.
Probably know others who could also be interested in it.

So put links to YOUR book in your other books.
Then they can copy or send it to others.

Put those links at the end of your book.
They have read your book.
So are more likely to share the experience with others they know.

Your link might look something like this:
Your book title.
Maybe you know someone who might be interested in THIS book?
If so please let them know about these links:
Then they can decide for themselves.

This link is to the ebook version:
http://www.amazon.com/dp/B07SH1GCHP

This is a link to the book:
http://www.Amazon.com/dp/1070839779

Write more books!
Then links to **ALL** your books can be in **ALL** your books.

What can you write about?
Well anyone who has bought **AND** read your first book.
Could be interested in a book about **YOU**.

So your story will probably be the next book you write AND publish.
This should also be an easy book to write.

Maybe someone is also interested in this book?
So let them know about the links.
I have done this except is it **MY** book rather than yours.

This link is to the ebook version of my book:
http://www.Amazon.com/dp/B07RRKZNZ8

This is a link to the paperback book:
http://www.Amazon.com/dp/1097675262

I have written other books too.
Some people you know might want to know about them?
So I have included their links too.

One book is Coach Creativity Skill.
Do you know anyone interested in how creativity can be developed?
Learn how to develop creativity in any group who meet regularly

Use this link to the book that shows how:
http://www.Amazon.com/dp/1797522655

Or this link to an identical ebook:
http://www.Amazon.com/dp/B07P46Z5M7

Another book is An Art Program.
Do you know anyone interested being the artist THEY want to be?
You can even teach someone to be the artist THEY want to be?!

Here is a link to a book that can help you:
http://www.Amazon.com/dp/1731347324

An alternative is to use this link to an ebook:
http://www.Amazon.com/dp/B07KK3Y9F5

I have an educational, art and business background.
I have also written books on these topics.
Some people you know might be interested in knowing about them?
So I have included their links just in case.

An introductory book is Preparation Tools.
It's for anyone who wants to prepare for a career as an artist?

This link is to a book that outlines what you need to do:
http://www.amazon.com/dp/B07SGPZC2Z

This ebook link covers the same information:
http://www.Amazon.com/dp/B07P5K1LH2

AMAZON MARKETING:

How do people buy your book using Amazon.com resources?
What do they have to do?

Customers buy your books as a retail sale.
If they want to buy your eBook "Boot Camp" they can purchase it here:
https://www.Amazon.com.au/dp/B009AKVLQI

If people have questions on how to buy a book.
They can use Amazon.com Kindle Customer Support links:
https://www.Amazon.com/clicktocall
https://www.Amazon.com/clicktochat

Find Amazon.com tips for marketing your book and increasing sales:
https://kdp.Amazon.com/self-publishing/help?topicId=A37SMD4NYVZDI7

KDP Print offers a fixed 60% royalty rate on paperback books.
If sold on any Amazon.com website.
Estimated royalty is 60% of your list price minus printing cost.
Not counting any applicable taxes or withholding:

Royalty = 60% List Price - Printing Costs - Tax or Withholding.
Printing cost depend on where the book was ordered from.
Costs vary depending on page count and ink type (black ink or color ink).
Trim size, bleed settings, and cover finish don't affect printing cost.

To calculate your printing cost, visit Amazon.com
Help page:https://kdp.Amazon.com/help?topicId=ATZHCE8PIQQR5

For Interior & paper type "Black ink & cream paper" and 100 pages.
The printing cost will be:
Fixed Cost + (Page Count * Per Page Cost) = Printing Cost.
$2.15 = Printing Cost.

Minimum List Price is the lowest retail price you can set.
If publishing your paperback through KDP Print.

KDP Print uses a Minimum List Price.
To ensure your royalties from paperback sales always cover printing costs.
Your paperback's Minimum List Price = Printing Cost / Royalty Rate (60%).
Your paperback's Minimum List Price = 2.15/60% = $3.58.

You can set and change list prices by marketplace.
Provided they're higher than the minimum list price.
Based on Printing Cost / Royalty Rate.
And lower than maximum list price ($250 (US), €250 (EU) or ¥30,000 (JP)).

For instance, if you set the list price at $5.99.
Royalty will be:
60% of List Price - Printing Costs - Taxes or Withholding = Royalty.
Thus 60% (5.99) - $2.15 = $1.44.

More on calculating printing cost, visit Amazon.com Help page.
https://kdp.Amazon.com/help?topicId=ATZHCE8PIQQR5

DISTRIBUTION:

Expanded distribution.
White paper is 6" x 9".
Make sure your list price exceeds minimum list price threshold.

How is a title enabled on Amazon.com marketplace.
For help:
https://kdp.Amazon.com/help/topic/GQTT4W3T5AYK7L45

Set up the book for a low price initially.
Later increase the price of your books when you wish to do it.

CREATE AN AUTHOR PAGE:

Create an Author Page through Author Central:
Then readers can get information about you and your work.
Sign in to Author Central on Amazon.com or on Amazon.com.co.uk.

Use Author Central to upload your picture, add a biography.
Also view and edit your bibliography.
Create a blog to contact direct to readers.

What if you already have an Author Page?
Make sure you claim all of your books, including this one.
Readers can search your book on Amazon.com website
They can use the book title name or your author name.

When they search on Amazon.com with the author's name.
Products are in order based on popularity, availability, and other factors.
They are a mix of most popular products in various product categories.

Creating a compelling author page takes a few minutes.
But it helps readers learn more about you and your books.
https://authorcentral.Amazon.com/gp/help/contact-us

MORE RESOURCES:

To promote your book and reach more readers:
Amazon.com offers merchandising programs :
Including ten ways to market your book.

Enroll your book in KDP Select,
An optional program for you to reach more readers and earn more money.

When you enroll a title in KDP Select.
It will be included in Kindle Unlimited .
For buyers in U.S., U.K., Germany, Spain, Italy, France, Brazil, Canada, Mexico, and India.
AND the Kindle Owners' Lending Library (KOLL).
For customers in the U.S., U.K., France, Germany, and Japan.

You can also choose between two promotional tools:
Kindle Countdown Deals or a Free Book Promotion - learn more, click here.

If you submit a manuscript how can you delay publishing?
Until I am at the conclusion of my marketing or for any other reason?

You plan to start selling at $10 – is that above the minimum price?
Your plan is to make it available at that low price for the first week only.
Then move it up for the next three weeks to $20.
After that set a final price of $30 - is this possible?

Save the title in draft status and publish the book at any time.
Once you publish the book.
It takes 72 hours to show up on the Amazon.com website.

Once you published your book.
It can take up to 30 days for a paperback book to be available.

Because your book's detail page builds in stages.
Your completed page and information may not appear all at once.

MORE COSTS:

Are 30% royalty AND 40% for sales to libraries etc.
KDP Print has a 60% royalty on books sold on an Amazon.com website.

But if you enable Expanded Distribution for your paperback.
The royalty rate is 40% of the book's list price.
Effective in the distribution channel at the time of purchase.
Less printing costs, applicable taxes, and withholding.

The estimated royalty of a book which has enabled Expanded Distribution:
Find the paperback on your Bookshelf.
On PAPERBACK ACTIONS menu, select Edit Paperback Rights & Pricing.
Select the territories for which you hold distribution rights.
Enter list price.
The pricing grid automatically updates printing cost and estimated royalty.

Can I give away a few (maybe 5) FREE copies?
If so how is that arranged?

Can I give away copies of my ebook?
Kindle Gifting is only supported on Amazon.com
The "Buy for Others" feature may gift one or multiple copies of any book.

If the book is:
Available in the country or region where the buyer lives.
Available on Amazon.com, rather than an individual country or region site.
Not available for free.
Not a pre-order.

To gift a book that doesn't meet these conditions.

Buy a gift card equal to the value of the book.
Suggest the recipient to buy the book with the gift card.

For details on Buy for Others see:
https://kdp.Amazon.com/help/topic/G200652260

For paperback books Amazon.com doesn't have this option.
To give away 5 copies buy author copies of your book as soon as it's live.
Then give them away.

For more information about author copies visit:
https://kdp.Amazon.com/help/topic/A3QUNMQXLDODOE

E: MORE AMAZON.COM HELP:

Before a book is published it should be formatted correctly.
If the book is **NOT** formatted correctly.
A previewer will highlight errors which need to be fixed.

If you recently started a new paperback title with KDP.
Additional help with paperback interior or cover file creation is available.

Check Amazon.com's formatting resources:
Paperback Essentials webinar.
For manuscript formatting tips and answers to your questions.
Watch a recording and check out the FAQ's.
https://kdp.Amazon.com/en_US/help/topic/G202193670#paperback_form atting

Look at KDP Build Your Book.
This is a step-by-step guide with videos and a downloadable PDF.
You can turn a manuscript in Microsoft Word into a PDF.
Ready to be uploaded to KDP:
https://kdp.Amazon.com/help/topic/G202145400?ref_=kdpgp_build_mail

If you have problem in formatting your content file.
Use the paperback template.

Download pre-formatted paperback manuscript templates from:
https://kdp.Amazon.com/help/topic/G201834230
Select a blank template or template with sample content in your trim size.

Templates with sample content include:
Front matter, chapters, headers, and page numbers.
Templates are adjustable to meet your preferences or book specifications.

If copying and pasting from an existing document.
Formatting from that document can be copied.

That can cause formatting problems in the templates.
To prevent this.
When pasting into the new document right-click.
From the Paste Options.
Choose to "Keep Text Only" when you paste.
This removes any formatting from the original source.

Amazon.com recommends page numbers only for blank templates.
Sample Content templates have page numbers inserted.
So making changes to those can cause problems.

Does your manuscript images/graphics "bleed" to the page edge?
If so you'll need to increase the trim size.
Add 0.125" to the width and 0.25" to the height.
For example, if the trim size is 6" x 9", set the page size to 6.125" x 9.25".
You could make the page content smaller instead.

Follow these direction to change the template page size:
1. In the "Page Setup" section of the Layout tab, click Size.
2. Select More Paper Sizes. This will open a dialog box.
3. Enter the book trim size, including bleed, into Width and Height fields.
4. In Preview section, select Whole document from Apply to menu.
5. Click OK.
This will resize your pages and change your page count.

For instructions to use the templates visit Amazon.com Help page:
https://kdp.Amazon.com/help/topic/G201834230

For troubleshooting the Previewer identifies, click Help here:

https://kdp.Amazon.com/help/topic/G201834260

Also check out KDP University, for more resources:
https://kdp.Amazon.com/en_US/help/topic/G200783400

Try KDP Jumpstart, an end-to-end guide.
It helps you turn your finished manuscript into a published book.
KDP experts created this step-by-step guided approach.
To help authors self-publish easily and effectively.
Use the industry advice in KDP Jumpstart and put your best book forward!

Learn more about KDP Jumpstart:
https://kdp.Amazon.com/help/topic/G202187740

Add a blank page in a Word document use the "insert" tab in Word.
Place cursor at bottom of the page where you want to insert a blank page
Click on the "Insert" tab
Click "blank page"

If you insert a fleuron (section divider).
Which is the three decorative elements like asterisks or diamonds.
It will be for aesthetics only and will not create a blank page.

A blank page forced by "pushing" the text down using the enter key,
You could cause formatting issues.
It is best to insert, the page to create a clean transition.
Also you do not need visible page numbers on blank pages.

Blank pages before your title page.
Can be included in you manuscript and at the end of the document.
It is possible to delete blank pages that have been added unintentionally.
Highlighting the page and then press delete on your keyboard.
You may have to try this a few times but it should remove the page.

Is the table of contents included with this document?
The table of contents could directly relate to the section/page headings. In terms of the style of formatting each section/page/chapter heading has.

Create your file to begin with in Word.
Then use the Kindle Create Add in to convert the file for Kindle.

To disable or remove an add-in follow these steps:
Click File > Options > Add-ins.

Towards the bottom of the window, it says:
Manage, click the Go button.
In the dialog box, select the add-ins you want to disable or remove.
To disable the add-in, just uncheck the box in front of its name.

If you are creating the paperback version.
Just Microsoft Word to then be able to save your file as a PDF.

Copy from the corrupted file.
Paste it into a Notepad document.
Then copy from Notepad and paste into Word.
This should remove any formatting errors embedded into the old Word file.

EVEN MORE HELP:

If you start a new paperback title with KDP.
If you'd like additional help with paperback interior or cover file creation.
Check Amazon.com formatting resources:

Paperback Essentials webinar.
For manuscript formatting tips and answers to your questions.
Watch a recording and check out the FAQ's.
https://kdp.Amazon.com/en_US/help/topic/G202193670#paperback_form
atting

KDP Build Your Book.
A step-by-step guide with videos and a downloadable PDF.
Turn a manuscript in Microsoft Word to a PDF ready to upload to KDP:
https://kdp.Amazon.com/help/topic/G202145400?ref=kdpgp_build_mail

Download pre-formatted paperback manuscript templates.
They are on the Help page:
https://kdp.Amazon.com/help/topic/G201834230

Select a blank template or one with sample content to your trim size.
Templates with sample content.
Include front matter, chapters, headers, and page numbers.

All templates are adjustable.
So they meet your preferences or book specifications.
If copying and pasting from an existing document.
Formatting from that document can be copied.
This can cause formatting problems in the templates.

To prevent this, when pasting into the new document, right-click.
From the Paste Options choose to "Keep Text Only" when you paste.
This removes any formatting from the original source.

Amazon recommend adding page numbers only for blank templates.
Sample Content templates have page numbers inserted.
So making changes to those can cause problems.

Some manuscripts images or graphics 'bleed" to the page edge.
If it does, you'll need to increase the trim size.
Add 0.125" to the width and 0.25" to the height.
So if your trim size is 6" x 9", set the page size to 6.125" x 9.25".
But you could reduce the image or graphics

Follow the below direction to change the template page size:
In the "Page Setup" section of the Layout tab, click Size.
Select More Paper Sizes. This will open a dialog box.
Enter book trim size, including bleed, into "Width" and "Height" fields.
In "Preview" section, select Whole document.
From the "Apply to" dropdown menu.
Click OK. This will resize your pages and change your page count.

For instructions to use the templates visit Amazon's Help page:
https://kdp.Amazon.com/help/topic/G201834230

For troubleshooting problems the Previewer identifies.
Check Amazon's Help page here:
https://kdp.Amazon.com/help/topic/G201834260

Also check out KDP University, for more resources:
https://kdp.Amazon.com/en_US/help/topic/G200783400

Use KDP Jumpstart.
It's a guide for making a finished manuscript a published book.
KDP experts created this step-by-step guided approach.
To help authors self-publish easily and effectively.

To learn more about KDP Jumpstart go to:
https://kdp.Amazon.com/help/topic/G202187740

To add a blank page in your Word document.
Use the "insert" tab in Word.
Place the cursor at the bottom of the page where you want a blank page
Click on the "Insert" tab then Click "blank page".

Blank pages before your title page.
Can be included within your manuscript.
And also at the end of the document.

It is possible to delete blank pages added unintentionally.
Highlight the page and then press delete on your keyboard.
You may have to try this a few times but it should remove the page.

If the table of contents is NOT included with the document.
The table of contents could directly relate to the section/page headings.
In terms of the style of formatting each section/page/chapter heading has.

To add the table of contents to the document.
Attach the updated WORD DOCUMENT to your email reply.
Then specify an exact location that the heading is not appearing correctly.
Amazon.com will investigate further other problems with the interior file.

Once Amazon.com gets a single file formatted correctly.
They can see about changing the format to PDF.
So you can upload for the paperback on your account.

If, you create your file to begin with in Word.
Then use the Kindle Create Add in to convert the file for Kindle.
If that file is corrupted you need to recreate the file.

To disable or remove an add-in follow these steps:
Click File > Options > Add-ins.
Towards the bottom of the window, where it says Manage.
Click the Go button.

In the dialog box, select the add-ins you want to disable or remove.
To disable the add-in, just uncheck the box in front of its name.

If you are creating the paperback version of this title.
You do not need to use the Kindle Create add in.
Simply Microsoft Word to then be able to save your file as a PDF.

If you are able to access the document.
But you can tell that there are problems with the font.
Or something about the file is corrupted.
You can create a new word document.
Then paste the content into that new document.

An alternative is to copy from the corrupted file.
Paste it into a Notepad document.
Then copy from Notepad and paste into Word.

TROUBLE-SHOOTING:

Open MS Word > file > options.
Under start up options uncheck.
"Show the Start screen when this application starts."
Please save the changes by selecting OK.
Please reboot your system and launch MS word.
In MS Word, go to: File -> Options -> Add-Ins.

A dialog box appears
This dialog box contains four sections:
Active Application Add-ins
Inactive Application Add-ins
Document related Add-ins
Disabled Application Add-ins

Find "Kindle Create Add-in for Microsoft Word" in the Add-in Dialog.

Inactive Application Add-ins:
Kindle Create Add-in for Microsoft Word in Inactive Application Add-ins.
Select COM Add-ins from Manage drop-down list at the bottom of page.
Click Go.
In the COM-Add-ins window that appears, click the check box:
Kindle Create Add-in for Microsoft Word.
This should move the Add-in to Active Application Add-ins section.
Close the dialog box to find Kindle Tab in MS word.

Disabled Application Add-ins:
Kindle Create Add-in for Microsoft Word in Disabled Application Add-ins.
Select Disabled items from the Manage drop-down-list and click go.
Select Kindle Create Add-in for Microsoft Word and click Enable.

The add-in will be listed under Inactive Application Add-ins.
Follow the steps listed above to activate the add-in.

Or uninstall and reinstall the application using the following steps:
Save your document and uninstall Kindle Create Add-in.
Go to: Control panel -> Programs and Features:
(https://support.microsoft.com/en-
us/search?query=programs%20and%20features)

Restart the system, download and install Kindle Create Add-in:
https://kdp.Amazon.com/en_US/help/topic/G202131100
Check if the issue is resolved.

If not, send Amazon.com the following log files.
Go to C:\[PROGRAM FILES]*\Amazon.com\KindleAddIn
Zip/Attach and share the file named KindleCreateAddIn.vsto.log
KindleCreateAddIn.log file from
C:\ProgramData\Amazon.com\KindleAddIn\logs

Copy and paste the above location in the address bar of any folder.

PAYMENT.

There is an option to switch to Direct Deposit for royalties.
If earned in the Australian marketplace.
This also applies to other countries as well.
Direct Deposit does not require you to meet the minimum threshold.

In all Marketplaces, Amazon pays royalties every month.
Approximately sixty (60) days following the end of the calendar month.
In which your royalties meet the payment threshold,
Royalties accrue on your account.
Until the total in each marketplace has reached the minimum threshold.

BOOKS SOLD:

To see a breakdown of which books and editions (paperback/eBook).
Make up the sales showing in your reports.
Click "generate report" at the bottom of the page.
This option will create an excel spreadsheet with more detail.

Will this link still work in a month's time?
Or does it expire like the link about where to find the information?
The link to your detail page won't expire.
Even if you make any changes to your book, the link will remain the same.

Where to find the "ASIN" details.
You can use the following format to post a link to your book:
http://www.Amazon.com/dp/ASIN

Just replace the word "ASIN" with the specific ASIN for your book.
You can find the ASIN in your KDP Bookshelf below the book title.
OR on the books detail page under "Product Details."

For Amazon.com de link is:
https://www.Amazon.com/dp/B07KDLFDZS

For Amazon.com.au the link will be:
https://www.Amazon.com.au/dp/B07KDLFDZS

Use the same link for your paperback book.
Then replace the word "ASIN" with the ISBN-10 for your book.
Which you can also find on the book's detail page under "Product Details.

To see how to link to your book on international Kindle Stores, visit:
https://kdp.Amazon.com/help?topicId=A1CT8LK6UW2FXJ

SUCCESS.

Success seems mythical, something like the Holy Grail.
The Crusaders of old travelled the world seeking it.
For authors the Holy Grail is to publish a book.
Then create major sales and build an income.

So how will you know you are a successful author?
That's for you to decide but consider these comments:

'Strong self-discipline and intelligent self-management are in my view the fundamental building blocks for all success.' (p77)

There will be disappointments along the way, that's how we learn. Each disappointment is a test of your commitment. They also add to your experience and strength. In the end your commitment is the key to success.
(Don Talbot – Australian swimming coach in "Nothing but the best")

If you are to be successful then you need to be well organized!
Elite athletes reap rewards by investing in themselves, so should authors.
BUT if you put it off it will never happen!

Eventually you blend elements and possibilities for success.
But there can be no half measures.
Either do it or forget it!
If you want to be a successful author then you must do the job properly.

You can gain knowledge.
But until you acquire experience and act on that knowledge.
You won't move ahead but will stay at your present state!

This is won't happen straight away.
It won't even happen at all!

Unless you know why you need a professional approach to your career.

The way of the leisure author will not get you there!
In a manner not previously possible you can set up your future earnings.
It will take time and a little money in the beginning.
If you wait until Christmas, next year, whenever the 'right' time to start is,
All that happens is the whole process is delayed.
There needs to be much work done.

With little actual expense initially, a start can be made if time is there.
You will build, or maybe re-building, the foundations of your author journey!
Possibly other things might need to be foregone, delayed or accelerated.
To facilitate a speedy transition to this new phase of your author career.

To be a successful author then writing well is not sufficient.
Many authors do that!
You also need to be successful at marketing and that's quite different!
In particular to take advantages of opportunities presented by Amzon.com.

Jumpstart is an end-to-end guide from Amazon.com.
It show you how to turn your finished manuscript into a published book.
KDP experts created this step-by-step guided approach.
It helps authors self-publish easily and effectively.

F: MY BOOK EXAMPLE

Ideas in this book are from my personal background and experience.
A little of which has been republished for you.

This book does NOT cover activities involving my family.
Naturally, like all families we have done many things.
However they are things we share rather than share with others.

I live in Wagga Wagga in Australia.
I've lived here since 1977, so am comfortable in this city of 65,000 people.
It's an environment with both strengths and weaknesses.

On the one hand:
I'm not located in the major art centres of my country.
So I'm out of touch with the current art scene there.
I'm independent and provide an alternative for those who feel the need.

In recent years, e-mail has eliminated the distance dramatically.
I'm in touch with people all over the world.
I've also found that the art culture is much the same everywhere.
So there is interest in my views as a result.

Am I an artist?
Yes I do paint, and have had many one man exhibitions (22 actually).
These days I spend most of my time writing articles and other stuff.
I do not paint anywhere near as much as I once did.

So now I'm probably a writer who paints sometimes. MY WRITING STYLE.

One reader commented about my writing style.
He thought it was probably best suited to using with a website.
Others liked the style for they found it easy to understand.
I call my method Easy-scan and I have used it for many years.

Easy-scan evolved from my experience in writing in newspapers.
I began a part-time career as a journalist back in the 1960's.
In those days I wrote about hockey for the Parkes Champion Post (6 years).
I also wrote on cricket for the Dubbo Liberal newspaper at that time.
More recently for 20 years I wrote on art for the Wagga Daily Advertiser.
The regular weekly article was called "Art Scene"

But I have also written in magazines.
Some had a national circulation such as the Hockey Circle in Australia.
I have written in is the Australian Artist magazine - monthly from 1995
I write bi-monthly articles in the International Artist magazine - 2002.

Naturally Art Professional newsletters are in this format too.
A Kindle series of books is in Easy-scan format as were my four websites.
As you now know Preparation Tools (this book) is in that style as well.

Easy-scan is written talking NOT academic writing.
It is me having a conversation with the reader (you).
So when people reviewed chapters of the book this is what they did.
They did not have to correct the spelling - that was done by a spellcheck.

Grammar is not important in a conversation either, for we just talk.
This book, like most others these days, was written on a computer.
That means it is easy to shift things around.
So as I write I often shift parts elsewhere.
Thus their main task is to identify where I have repeated myself.

Teaching is part of the business of art.
So teaching is a commercial option for an artist.
This can be an addition to painting or any other artistic activity.

Not all artists want to teach but many do.
You choose whether to become involved or not.

BUT if you do you're in business and business principles apply to teaching.

I was a teacher before I became an artist.
But you can do it the other way around and I've done that too.

I developed art related courses both in my gallery days and since.
There are many who specialize in helping people understand art.
Spend more time teaching and earn more money that way.

Of course you can teach less and paint more.
John Hill (UK) thinks it's hard to paint and teach without compromise.
John says successful teaching requires creativity and hard work.

Often this is to the detriment of the teacher's own art.
Students influence technique, style, palette, subject matter of the teacher.

But some well established artists also teach.
Their teaching is usually based on their personal painting skills.

Whether to specialize or not, is a choice artists have.
Anyone can specialize.
Maybe a media (oils), particular subjects (portraits}, or style (impressionist}.

Teachers can do the same.
But what you can't do is both specialize and not specialize.
The beginner artist tends to try all ideas, media, subjects and so forth.

A beginning teacher often does this too!
They have to do this to find out what they like and do best.
Some artists even do this for a very long period.
They become life-long students. Nothing wrong with that either!

Many people discover certain things interest them more than others.
Maybe it's various combinations of media, colours, or subjects.

They tend to follow this interest.
Nothing wrong with that either.
Teachers can do the same.
Because of their focus, they get better at their specialty.
They apply knowledge and experience with great depth and understanding.

I met many artists when I had my gallery.
Quite a few of them said they'd love an agent so all they had to do was paint.

I never met any agents although they do exist but none visited me.
So I gave the idea of an artist having an agent some thought.

Delegation is the key to leveraging yourself.
You get other people to do things for you.
In business there is an awareness of the importance of delegation.
It's lacking in art as we tend **NOT** to think of ourselves as employers.

Used effectively it's possible to increase income and free time as well!
If you do what you do best; delegate or discontinue anything else.
Time on tasks of lesser value is inefficient investment of time and energy.
Delegate any tasks that can be performed by a person earning less.

That frees time to focus energy on tasks worth $50 per hour or more.
Delegate to people who have competence in a specific field.
People who know more are more efficient and carry out tasks in less time.

In my case it's worth paying an accountant.
Define the task clearly.

What is your intended outcome?
Be clear about what you want the person to do.
You'd like an agent, but what exactly do you expect them to do?
Then should you start looking for someone who can and is willing to do that.

Find the person for the task.
Ask THEM to repeat the details of the task IN WRITING.
Is their description an accurate description of what you want accomplished?
If not explain the differences in detail.
AGAIN submit their understanding IN WRITING.

The writing step helps enormously in achieving buy-in.
It also helps to make sure you get the outcome you want.
Otherwise they'll do what they think you want, which may not be the same.
Discuss and get agreement on the resources to achieve the task.

There's a major problem if you've hired an agent.
AND they submit invoices for travel and accommodation.
But delegation turns out, keep your word regarding consequences.
These steps could be used by someone who wants to commission a work.
Convert the steps into a written guarantee.

My art classes at school largely consisted of pastel drawing.
Everyone drew an orange, or an apple, or some other still life object.
Probably pupils everywhere at that time did much the same thing.

I liked those lessons.
Strangely enough I haven't used pastels since.
I think I didn't like the feel of the actual pastel in my hand, but I'm not sure.
But I certainly admire them and have bought quite a few by other artists.

Ever since I remember, I drew things, but I don't do that now either.
Initially much of it was copied.
I recall, in primary school days, copying sailing ships and designing cars.
I doodled a lot, drew on the back of books and just enjoyed the experience.
It didn't seem anything special, just something I could do.

I didn't even do art at high school.
At Teachers College I had my first art lessons.
It was also when I first painted.

I enjoyed this and did quite well at it.
Now when I look at those early paintings, they're not very good at all.
This ended when I began my first career, as a primary school teacher.
It was a bit of a shock.

National Service during Teachers College had left me somewhat deaf.
That made my teaching experiences difficult.
I persevered and developed some competency.
But without becoming outstanding in any way.

I hadn't actually give much thought to actually being a teacher.
Although my father was one.
Gradually I realized I was only marking time as a teacher.
I should do something about it.

I loved my life, but teaching and school, was the down side.
In hindsight my deafness was, a major contributor to this problem.
I contemplated other careers, but wasn't qualified for anything.
Except teaching.

I'd have gone, without hesitation, into sports administration.
But those were different times and that was a non-paying choice only.

But life outside school was very enjoyable.
I played sport, particularly hockey and cricket, but others as well.
That's when I bought my first sports car.
Sometimes I even went out with young women.

My involvement with art was minimal.
Occasionally I drew on the blackboard.
Also I sometimes sketched children in the class.
As well I designed various sporting awards.

Gradually I realized I was only marking time as a teacher.

I thought perhaps I could become an artist.

It wasn't a dream, or something I always wanted to do.

Just an idea in the back of my mind.

One day I saw a promotion.

Primary school teachers could retrain as secondary art teachers.

It was an art course, as the students were already qualified teachers.

I thought this might be an avenue to escape from the classroom.

Perhaps this way I could really become an artist?

The course was part-time so I would still be teaching and earning money.

That meant little financial risk.

Some people seemed to think I was 'artistic' so I made enquiries.

Almost instantly I found myself enrolled for the following year.

With considerable encouragement from my principal in that direction.

This might solve some of my problems (and his too).

But it meant a move to Sydney which I was not keen on.

I'm basically a country boy.

But once the wheels started turning there was no stopping them.

I duly became an art student.

At a four year course, four nights a week and on Saturday mornings too.

So I enrolled in a course at the East Sydney Technical College.

I also had to move from Parkes to Sydney.

During the week I was still teaching, although at a high school.

I applied myself to the course at the National Art School.

It was to be my ticket out of teaching and I'd moved to Sydney to do it.

I had no intention of wasting any of that opportunity.

Most of my new classmates were more relaxed about it than me.

But I was there to learn.

If I did this well enough, perhaps I could be an artist instead of art teacher.

Consequently I became quite involved with art, particularly my own.

Eventually it joined sport as a major part of my life.

I was easily the most naïve of all my classmates.
I had never previously been in a gallery.
I'd only heard of the most famous artists (da Vinci, van Gogh, Monet,).
But surprisingly I was actually one of the best drawers!
I found that I could paint quite well too.

I learnt what I could, and improved from my basic beginning.
But for me art was something confined to the art school.
I spent weekends playing sport, rather than attending art exhibitions.
But I had a look at the Archibald and Wynne Prize exhibitions each year.

At the end of the year I was quite pleased with my results.
I passed everything, with credits and distinctions too.
Along with several others I was one of the top students.

The next year was similar.
Most other students did whatever necessary to get through the course.
But I was still trying to learn.
Again several distinctions were my reward.
This time in a different combination of subjects.

But now there was a nagging feeling too.
Maybe I should be doing even better for my efforts.
It was just something tucked away in the back of my mind.
Rather than any major concern.

As in most tertiary institutions, the quality of lecturer varied.
In the third year one 'lecturer/teacher' was different from the others.
The others had Ideas, passed on knowledge, were keen for us to learn.
They generally did the kinds of things you'd expect teachers to do.

There were slight exceptions.
One actually used our work as material for a book.
Another was keen for us to do well.

So he'd take home unfinished student paintings.
Then work on them to ensure a good result.
Fortunately this didn't happen for me.
But the teacher who was different did none of this.
He was a well-respected artist but a hopeless teacher.
He appeared for his classes and suggested something for us to do.

He had few comments about how we did it or what was done.
Quite often he had been drinking and wasn't really able to offer much.
In addition he often arrived late and sometime left early too.

There were even occasions when he didn't arrive at all.
My fellow students also arrived late, went early or stayed at the local pub.
Even some combination of these, including not even coming.
Except for the intoxication part, although they did go to the pub.

I kept coming even though I had to spend a lot time driving.
I was teaching at Carlingford in north-western Sydney.
In evening peak hour traffic to Darlinghurst in the eastern suburbs.
Then drive home west to Parramatta each evening.
It certainly was tempting not to come too.
But I was still motivated by the artistic career, which beckoned.

So I kept turning up, still keen to learn.
Eventually I was the only student present (it was a small class).
With no lecturer to learn from I wasn't prepared to waste my time.
But I didn't know what to do.

The first time this happened I stared at my blank canvas for a while.
Then I looked at my paints and noticed a tube of Indian red.
I hate Indian red, I thought, so let's use up some of that.
I mixed the paint with plenty of turps and looked at the canvas again.

I still didn't know what to do.
So I flung the paint onto the canvas in random splashes.

A little later I decided to join the dots of paint using lines.
I considered the shapes created and thought I should colour some in.

So I painted in some of the shapes with more Indian red.
Some white was added and more shapes painted.
I continued working on the painting, but more quickly.
It developed into quite a reasonable abstract painting.

I don't know what happened to it.
I wish I still had it for that was my first real painting.

Next week it was the same situation again.
However, I decided against flicking the paint this time.
I shut my eyes and made random marks on the canvas.
Then continued painting with the shapes that resulted.
This was my second painting and I also learned something.

I learned in those two lessons (with no teacher) how to get started.
I learned that it doesn't really matter what you do at the start.

The most important thing is to actually do something.
Your mind works better when there's something for it to work with.
A blank canvas is really uninspiring and for many people inhibiting.
We know great masterpieces were painted on similar blank canvases.
Often we try to solve all our artistic problems before we start.
That's generally too hard.
It's usually unnecessary too for most can be worked out along the way.
These two lessons were life-changing events for me.

I continued with my course and learned an even more important lesson.
This isn't just how to get started on a painting;
It's how to get started with anything.

IT'S A RULE OF LIFE!

I continued with this attitude in the fourth and final year of my course.
The lesson from the hopeless teacher's class, has guided my life.
Doing something, even if it's random, is better than doing nothing.
You can learn and grow.
It doesn't matter what you do, the most important thing is to actually start.
Once you begin, you can alter or change what you've done.
But at least something happens.
So you can, and usually will, build on it.

I'm actually doing it now with this book.
You can do it with your book.

Often we try to solve all our problems before we start.
That's generally too hard.

Perfectionism is a waste of time too.
Working things out along the way is better.
Then you embark on a process of continued improvement.
This will lead to highs never even imagined by the perfectionists.

This is also the Bill Gates (Microsoft) approach!
There is no need to procrastinate on anything.
One reason for this is once you act on an idea, it is tested in the real world.

Your idea is held up and inspected.
It will stand or fail, or maybe even both, but in different ways.
You can then take further action.
Modify those things that need modifying.
Develop those other things that can be developed.

Thus an idea is improved.
It can become greater than the original thought.
Which otherwise would remain as an untested idea.
Where you end up, won't be random.
It'll be considerably better than you could have imagined in the beginning.

It's better to do something and be wrong, than do nothing.
Mistakes can be corrected, and you learn what not to do at the same time.
With experience and confidence later starts improve on earlier ones.
But even then you must start.

A classmate, later a university lecturer with a Phd. in Art Education
Arthur said 'It's all right having fun and enjoying yourself.
But wait until the end of the year.
You have to do what they want you to do!'

I suppose generally he was right.
At most educational institutions you have to do what lecturers want.
Or you fail.

I thought about that briefly, but not for long.
I didn't really care, whether I passed or failed.
I was on my way to being an artist.
One thing I knew was being an artist was based on what you did.
Not whether you'd passed a course or not.

Many artists haven't even done formal courses.
Others have failed but it didn't matter!
I kept going as before, in spite of the well-intentioned advice.
I had a busy and productive year and my development moved nicely.

Eventually the end of the course came, and the exams arrived as well.
When the results came out I received distinctions in every subject.
Naturally I was very pleased and quite proud of the achievement.

A little further down the track I realized what had actually happened.
Examining students was the same as in every other art institution.
A student submits two or sometimes three works in each subject.
With printmaking a portfolio was required.

The works are then viewed by a panel of examiners.
They are specialists in a particular subject area.
One of them was the lecturer.
Each independently rank works from best to worst and allocated marks.
Then the group would compare results for the final mark.
They were faced with fairly similar works and one that was different.

If most students have 'done what they wanted you to do'.
Then their works will tend to be similar and somewhat like the lecturers.

The different one will be placed as best or worst.
With some skill and creativity a best place is more likely.
This is basically why I received those distinctions.

My work was different from my classmates!
I had to be judged best or worst, but I couldn't possibly be equivalent.

That's how it is in the art world too.
In medicine, or accountancy, I would've had an entirely different result.
So if you haven't gleaned the main point from my experience it is this:
In art it's more important to be different from other artists than the same.

You might consider briefly the situation in any craft form.
There the reverse is true - except you want to be better.

Now I was confident about myself as an artist.
I believed I could make a living from it.
So like many others I did what seemed to be logical.
I entered works in various art exhibitions with a view to selling them.
Winning was a possibility, but not as important to me as selling.

Again like many artists I packed up works and sent them off.
Mostly they came back, but occasionally a cheque would arrive.
Towards the latter part of this year I entered the Wynne Prize.
Many people visit that exhibition, including me.

The chance of selling could be better than other competitions I entered.

I did two large paintings which I delivered to the Art Gallery of NSW.
I was pleased when both works were hung.
But disappointed as neither sold.
I still have one and the other
I painted over.

In the following years my artistic endeavours were diverted.
I followed an educational pathway.
Entering art exhibitions became something in the past.

After ten years I opened an art gallery.
I exhibited other people's work.
I became aware there were artists who rated as a major achievement.
Having a work hung in the Wynne Prize.

Until then I had only thought of my entry as a failed sale opportunity.
I hadn't realized that it was actually an achievement.
If I had, I'd have entered again the following year and other years since.
Perhaps I could have become a winner?
But in fact I've never entered again.

You do different things according to your motivation and knowledge.
I entered the Wynne Prize because my motivation was selling.
If my motivation had been to win, then I would have continued exhibiting.

Decisions on superficial understandings can affect all that follows.
You really do owe It to yourself to weigh everything up all the time.
I'm not complaining because, in life there's always choices to be made.
The important thing is to make them and then get on with it.
Generally I have done that.

CONSULTING.

I was an art consultant for the NSW Department of Education.
That was instead of becoming a famous artist.
I was to help elementary and infants teachers improve their art teaching.

There was an assumption behind my appointment.
And also of others like me.
It was we knew about art and could pass this knowledge on to the teachers.
If we were successful then obviously they would do a better job.

There was an initial familiarization period.
I met many of my clients (teachers).

I also realized there was a major fallacy in this appointment assumption.
If I could teach them all I knew or even a fair bit.
They would be specialists, like me.

To raise standards in all areas of education.
The same process was needed in other areas thought worth developing.
There was indeed a range of other educational consultants.

To expect any teacher to be an expert in all fields is clearly unrealistic.
Like everyone else I thought teachers lacked knowledge about art.

Eventually I found that what they lacked were suitable teaching skills.
They were using one set of skills to teach everything.
These skills worked very well in some areas and not so well in others.

It was assumed in art, music, and dance teachers lacked knowledge.
In fact they were using inappropriate teaching methodologies.

However, there was another direction that could be pursued.
Although no one seemed to want to move this way.

How about changing art education.
So it could be taught by non-specialists?

I followed this path when I realized the error of the initial assumption.
There were some lucky breaks, blunders, and maybe even wisdom.

I also found out something about teachers that I was not expecting.
Anyone can teach art, music, and so on.
If they use more appropriate teaching methods
Particularly with young children.

Other areas covered in my book include:
      CRICKET:
      HOCKEY.
      COACHING HOCKEY.
      CARS:
      FRAMING.
      ART TEACHING:
      BOOKS.
      CREATIVITY.

Your book could eventually also cover multiple aspects of your life.

WHERE NEXT:

Perhaps this book could interest you now?

The Human Character is a background.
Just download this link.
http://www.amazon.com/dp/B08BDSDL9Z
The Human Character book.
http://www.amazon.com/dp/B09GRKCWMK

NOT NOW:

Perhaps one of these books could interest you then?

A simple way to start developing creativity.
If you are a parent, teacher or someone who meets a group regularly?
To learn exactly how - download from this link.
http://www.amazon.com/dp/B088T1KFQZ

Starting an art career Is NOW is harder than it ever was.
To help someone start – they download this link
http://www.amazon.com/dp/B088T7VJ76

This is the way most people start to become an artist!
To learn how - download from this link.
http://www.amazon.com/dp/B088Y1DPL6

My memories might interest you.
Find out what they are - download from this link.
http://www.amazon.com/dp/B088Y4RPL9

SEND TO

Know anyone interested in chocolate recipes?

If so they can download this link:

http://www.amazon.com/dp/B0882HK9Q9

Know anyone interested in THIS book?

They should download this link:

http://www.amazon.com/dp/B08BDSDL9Z

www.ingramcontent.com/pod-product-compliance
Lightning Source LLC
Chambersburg PA
CBHW020328290526
45785CB00007B/2963